The Halbert Copywriting Method

Part III- Editing

The Simple, Fast, and Easy Editing Formula That Forces Customers To Read Every Single Word You Write!

By Bond Halbert

Copyright Bond Halbert 2016

Table of Contents

Foreword – By Sam Markowitz

Intro

Why This Information is So Valuable

Why Listen To Me

Things To Know First

What This Book Is Not
What To Expect

Section One - Things To Know First
Editing Strategy
Time To Allow For Editing
5 Tips For Better Editing

When To Break The Rules of Grammar

Section Two - Helping Readers Decide To Dive In To Your Copy
Eye Relief

Break Up Long Paragraphs

Breaking Up Sentences
Punctuating Tips
Fonts, Backgrounds & Line Spacing

Formatting for Sales- Print

Inserting Subheads

Section Three - Editing For Clarity
The Trick To Finding Errors Professional Editors Miss
"That" Hunt
Big Word Hunting

Repeat Word Hunting

Transitions

Section Four - How To Keep Them Reading
Cliffhangers

Rearranging Sentences So Punch Is At The End

Section Five - How To Punch Up Copy

Highlighting Words & Phrases
How To Find and Insert Power Words
Qualifier Hunt

The Halbert "I" To "You" Formula
Using Technical Jargon For Authority
Move Answers Up

The "So What" Test

More Resources

Free Bonus!

If you email me proof you purchased this book, I'll send you a notepad with my editing checklist printed on each page.

Now this offer is only good for as long as supplies last but be warned.

The checklist is only a reminder of each part of the editing formula.

You still want to read every word of this short yet powerful book because in most cases I have added my own twists to many of the standard copy editing techniques and of course I have added a lot of brand new ways to punch up copy which have never been shared with the copywriting world.

To get your notepad visit http://bondhalbert.com/bonus

I'll also send you my other checklists as they become available and you can of course opt out of my copywriting club at any time.

Now let's get to the good stuff.

Foreword By Sam Markowitz

I am always looking for an edge.

I went to study and work with Gary Halbert the last year of his life precisely because that's what I wanted.

Two years after my apprenticeship, my copy was already producing tens of millions of dollars in sales.

One year with Gary gave me an edge I think otherwise could have taken me decades to achieve on my own. I am blessed.

Mindbogglingly…

Gary's son Bond has been learning from his father since Bond was 11 years old – an education spanning the course of decades with his dad.

This endowed him an understanding of Gary's work and teachings few can rival.

He wrote this book, based on patterns he found in the work of his dad and many of the other world's top copywriters he knows and he's studied.

The book is about editing - a subject that may not sound so 'sexy'. But we are looking for an edge, not *sexy*. And, I find personally, anything that gives me an edge… is *sexy*.

The more prospects who read your copy, the more sales you can make. Period.

Therefore, everything you can do to make it easy and seamless for your prospects to read your copy from beginning to end, the more sales you make.

That's why Gary used to spend a lot of time editing. I'm aware of times he would edit something he wrote *16 times*. He was after an edge. He was after perfection.

Now, Bond has consolidated all the best tips and tricks on editing copy into this one book.

Many are insightful way beyond just editing. They illustrate how great writers pine over every word, every nuance. (As example, see the tip *'Change a few "but"s to "yet"*)

There is great detail here. Things you may have never read before about editing.

When it comes to improving your copy, Bond has much to share and teach.

Everything he discusses is easy to understand, and more importantly, easy to put into use right away.

Add these tips and tricks to your arsenal today to give you a further edge.

Sam Markowitz- Professional Copywriter

Intro

This Editing Formula WILL Make Everything You Write So Much More Effective You Can Raise Your Rates!

What I'm going to share with you will give you an advantage over even the best copywriters on Earth but...

You need to know two things first.

First the bad news...

This magic formula only helps make your message more readable, engaging and exciting.

This formula can NOT make Eskimos want more ice.

All the power in your sales copy comes from what you are saying and knowing your audience... **not** *how* you say it. In other words... market research is much more important than any creative writing ability.

It takes marketing talent/experience to develop highly effective hooks, offers, and solutions from your research. The editing process which I'm going to thoroughly explain... is where all the professionalism comes into play.

Just remember... no amount of clarity will make a bad offer better. Selling the wrong products to the wrong people at the wrong time will result in more wasted energy and resources than poorly worded copy.

With that being said...

Here is the good news!

Why This Editing Formula Will Give You An Advantage over Other Copywriters

Few people know how to edit for sales copy. Schools mostly teach people how to write reports which are designed to pass on information to people forced to read it.

Students are taught to state a premise, offer 3-5 supporting arguments, and sum everything up into a nice package of information.

Plus, college graduates have been taught to write 50 pages on something which only requires 5 pages and they are also taught to boil down a whole philosophy into a one-page essay.

Nobody is taught how to be entertaining or keep people interested in what's being said.

Even in journalism, the articles are designed in such a way few people finish them because they give all the details you want to know up front. Only those with OCD or people with a personal interest in a story finish reading entire articles but... a copywriter has to get the reader to take action so they need a different approach.

Sales copy must suck the reader in, be super easy to read, evoke an emotional response and motivate customers to buy which is a whole different goal than almost any other kind of writing.

If using this formula helps just one prospect continue reading your copy, the book will have paid for itself but... the effect this formula has is already proven to be so powerful it can mean the difference between success and failure.

Let me give you some proof.

Once I wrote an email sales letter at the same time as another professional copywriter selling the exact same product.

His copy was radically different from mine so we split-tested the sales copy and we also did something I've never seen tested before.

Using this formula, I edited the other copywriter's work and all three sales messages were sent to the same list.

I'm happy to report the results prove the power of this formula.

The grammatically correct but unedited copy the other copywriter submitted was soundly defeated, but the other writer's copy (edited using this formula) pulled in about the same number of orders as my sales copy.

This PROVES The Editing Method Works Like A Magic Charm!

My copy slightly outperformed the other piece which can be put down to different selling points or an endless amount of small differences but...

Applying This Editing Formula Increased SALES 400%!

The fact that the editing formula was used in both the winners proves this formula keeps a lot more people reading.

Want more proof?

I use this formula in all my writing and the websites with my copy have much longer "time on site" stats than I have seen from anyone else. Sometimes as much as 19 minutes!

A few parts of this formula were developed by others and popularized by my father but a huge amount of this whole formula was developed by me and all these steps have never been put in one place before.

Oddly, I'm the perfect person to explain how to edit your copy for promotions and here's...

Why You Should
Listen To Me On
How To Edit Copy!

It's pretty well known that my father Gary C. Halbert was one of, if not *the* greatest copywriter in history.

He smashed sales records in a bunch of unrelated niches. The Prince of Print also gets credit for teaching more of today's top copywriters than any other person in history but being a member of Frank Sinatra's family doesn't mean you can sing like him.

My dad is famous for teaching other copywriters their craft and because of his book The Boron Letters, it's well known that he taught me all the ins and outs of his business since I was 11 years old and that's what I now do for a living.

Because of the access being Gary Halbert's son gave me, I have spent over 40 years reading, critiquing and analyzing the most effective copy in the world and more importantly...

According to personality tests, I have one trait which stands out as highly advanced and that trait is pattern recognition, so I don't even get credit for these techniques.

You see what I'm going to share with you isn't my brilliance. This editing formula is based on the patterns found in the work of the world's most effective copywriters and master salesmen born with a natural gift.

I did earn a degree in marketing and I have done more than my fair share of writing in college so I know the rules of grammar and more importantly, I know when to break them and soon, you will too.

Not only do I feed my family with the words I write but... I also teach other professional copywriters to take their game to the next level.

Highly paid wordsmiths in all niches come to me when they need a unique hook or solution but...

It's the editing phase where I show them how to inject a lot of hidden yet effective psychological patterns the legends (including my father) used but never shared because they themselves never dove that deep into their own natural ability.

I've heard every copywriting lesson known to man over and over again for a couple decades and I have never heard some of these formulas and patterns I saw in good copy explained by any copywriting guru and again this includes my legendary father.

The formulas I have created for research or writing post scripts, headlines and bullets all work like a charm and in this book you will see that same thought process applied to editing with the single goal of keeping the right prospects reading.

Once I started to share these advanced level concepts with other professional copywriters they were blown away because... they didn't think there was anything new to learn.

Now it is very important for you to also know...

What This Book Is NOT

This is not a continuation of the famous marketing book, The Boron Letters.

This is also NOT a complete copywriting course. If you want to make money writing promotions, you need to know a lot more than just how to edit copy until it is smooth as silk.

What You Can Expect

The goal of direct response sales copy is obviously to make sales. A great piece of copy grips the attention of people who come across the promotion. The copy must get them excited about the opportunity being offered and motivate them to take action with a sense of urgency so strong they can't wait to buy.

As, I said earlier, most of all the powerful key components of any good promotion come from the research phase where you decide what the message and offer are.

Once the hook, sales points, stories, headline and other components are all put down on paper or up on a screen, it's time to tweak the greased slide.

The idea behind the concept of the greased slide is this...

If anyone truly interested in what you offer starts reading the ad from the headline, beginning or the middle of the copy, they should effortlessly move from one paragraph to the next as though they were on a greased slide and can't stop falling from one line to the next.

Great copy makes the prospects forget they are reading. Potential buyers should become so emotionally involved in what is being said they forget the world around them and before they know it, they should have a burning desire to take action.

After we are done, you will know how to make your copy so smooth... any reader interested in your message will fall through it.

A little of the bit of The Halbert Editing Formula is very well known because my father shared his part but I have added over a dozen of my own twists and no matter how great your talent is, this WILL help you become so much better at writing copy you will be able to raise your rates so let's get started.

Section One

Things You Should Know First

This section explains the idea behind this editing method and what to expect.

In this section you will also find 5 tricks proven to make everything you write and edit better.

The Strategy Behind The Halbert Editing Method

One of the reasons Gary Halbert was such a great teacher is he repeated the most important lessons and I'm going to do the same right now.

Knowing what really excites your prospects comes from understanding your buyers so well you know what they want to buy, when they want to buy it, what they need to hear to make the decision to buy, who they want to buy from, what will make them rush to buy now and so on but...

Once you are ready to put all that information to use and it's time to tell the prospects about your really hot offer you want to cast a spell over the right prospects.

It's okay if we lose all the wrong prospects. In fact the sooner we lose the people who would never buy our products and service the better off we are.

We don't want haters to stick around and leave bad reviews on our YouTube sales videos and we don't want to pay for Alaskans clicking on ads for a one-day special offer at a waffle house in Mississippi but...

Assuming our headline and talking points are super exciting to the right people, we want the copy to suck the reader in, make them forget everything going on around them. We want to give the readers the only thoughts they will have about the offer.

We want to answer all of their concerns before they can even think of them.

We also want the true prospects to feel like there is no place they can stop reading without missing some vital piece of information which could make their lives better and we don't want the spell to be broken until after they buy!

This editing formula is designed to accomplish all those goals in just four stages.

The first stage helps the reader *decide* to read or listen to your copy. I'll explain this in the next chapter.

The second stage of the editing formula is aimed at making your messages so crystal clear anyone who can read will understand it.

The third part of the magic formula injects hidden psychology into your copy which keeps the prospect reading and fuels their desire to buy.

This is the stage that gives the reader the feeling they will miss out big if they stop reading and the techniques go way beyond using simple cliffhangers.

If this is done right your readers won't even think about anything other than what you want them to think until after they buy.

The fourth stage will show you how to inject hidden psychology and help you punch up your copy to make whatever you are selling as attractive as possible.

How Much Time To Allow For Editing

When it comes to writing any copy, the first stage is the most important, the most overlooked, and the best place to find the advantage over your competition.

I am of course talking again about marketing research which is beyond the scope of this book.

During this stage you will usually develop the big idea for your new promotion and that is the critical element to writing sales record crushing copy.

The biggest marketing triumphs and breakthroughs come from truly unique and effective hooks, offers, solutions or any combination of the three and the best breakthroughs come from really knowing your customers.

The magic in Domino's famous offer to deliver pizza in less than 30 minutes or it's free was brilliant because of the research, not the copy.

The offer could have been expressed in many different ways.

The words "We'll deliver your pizza in under 30 minutes or it's free" wasn't brilliant.

The offer was brilliant and the offer came from knowing people were sick of not knowing when their pizza would arrive.

Another point is it's important when you hit on a great offer to run with your promotion fast and hard.

A ton of pizza parlors started making 30 minute delivery guarantees but only one built a an empire on that unique offer.

In other words the attention jarring effect of any campaign loses steam over time people only remember the first person to get famous for running a 4 minute mile or climbing Mount Everest.

The most successful promotions usually have unique hooks, offers or solutions which were developed during the research phase.

If you want great advice on developing big ideas, grab my track from The Gary Halbert Letter All-Star Audio Series on the subject. It's cleverly labeled… The Big

Idea.

You can find the entire series at Halbertizing.com

After doing enough research to really understand your product or service and you really know what makes your customers tick it's time to develop that unique hook, offer or solution.

Then it is time for the copy dump.

The copy dump is when you finally put the conversation with a potential customer in your head and the offer in writing.

This first draft should be the shortest stage of all. It should be so rough you refuse to show it to anyone and it is like a diamond in the rough. It will not shine until it has been carefully cut and polished in the editing phase.

You should edit your copy until it is so smooth that… before the readers know it, they have finished reading every word and are eager to take action.

This editing phase should take up almost as much time as market research and the less unique your offer is, the more time you should put into the editing phase.

The best course of action is to make up a deadline (if you don't already have one) and then Divide the time into three equal sections.

The first phase is for research, the second is for brainstorming opening copy, bullets, strategizing and developing The Big Idea and putting it all down in a very rough draft.

The final phase is editing.

Since developing The Big Idea often comes from research and the copy dump is so quick, you will usually have a lot of extra time for research or editing but don't take too long.

It sucks to spend weeks perfecting a promotional idea that doesn't work.

That's right. Not every piece of copy is a winner, So any extra time to launch should be spent testing ideas.

To sum it up, editing should take about a third of the time you have until your deadline. Editing should never go on so long you are putting off testing different hooks.

Also, you should know...

Copy Needs To Be Edited Over and Over Again But... Using This Formula Gets Faster and Faster

Nobody, including the great Gary C. Halbert has been able to write great copy with only one edit.

There are <u>always</u> too many errors, rough spots or opportunities to punch up the copy to catch in one single pass but...

As you get more familiar with this editing formula, you will start fixing more errors each time you sit down to edit and... you will also slowly start to change the way you write to reflect what you discover in this book but no matter what...

Don't Think About The Editing Process When You Write

I'll explain why in the next chapter.

5 Tips For Better Writing & Editing!

Tip #1 Don't Apply This Formula While Writing

The rules from this formula will seep into your writing style over time but when you are pounding out that first draft of your copy, you never want anything disturbing the flow of your words and getting your ideas onto the screen or paper is more important when writing your first draft.

It's best to keep going and clean the text up later, but it's good to know applying the editing formula gets faster and faster as you start fixing more issues we are about to discuss every time you edit your copy.

Tip #2 Edit & Write in Complete Passes

You do NOT want to spot errors, fix them and then start re-reading from the top again.

I see amateurs do this all the time. Their copy starts off smooth because the beginning has been edited 20 times and the end falls apart because it was only looked at once by someone very tired of editing.

The reader will lose a little trust as they see more and more errors.

There is another reason to edit in complete passes and it's also why you should write in complete passes too.

We humans are emotional and moody people.

Every single day we wake up feeling more confident or a little more insecure than usual and this is especially true of business owners and copywriters.

One day you are on top of the world boasting about the greatness of your products and the next, you are worried about living up to what you wrote.

Your emotional attitude can mess up the editing process if you tone down half the bullet points on one day and punch up the ending on another day.

Your copy will be better if the level of excitement is strong throughout the entire copy.

Some writers simply avoid writing or editing unless they are feeling emotionally strong but professional writers don't always have that luxury.

If you edit the same copy on three different days it will have the right balance of punch which is... as exciting as possible without making promises so big the buyers will feel even slightly disappointed.

That being said, there are very rare instances where you may be working on a magalog or some other epic size sales letter. In instances where writing or editing in a complete pass is simply impossible, break up the copy into editable segments.

Magalogs lend themselves to being written like a book so breaking up the writing and editing task into chapters is easy.

With a super long sales letter try to segment the job into the following categories

- Opening copy
- Story telling
- Features & Benefits
- Closing

For what it's worth the opening and closing take the most time and talent so it's good to write those when you are feeling particularly sharp and confident.

Moving on...

Tip #3 Edit With Fresh Eyes

Let the copy rest between edits because you will catch more errors and do a much better job if you are not bleary eyed from looking at the same copy over and over again all day.

After making a complete editing pass, go do something else.

I never make more than two editing passes in one day which leads me to my next tip.

Tip #4 Borrow Fresh Eyes!

If the copy is very important, I ALWAYS have a trusted friend read my work and highlight any errors or places they get confused.

I'm fortunate enough to have a lot of copywriting buddies so I get what you would call very expensive professional help but...

Anyone you can get to read your sales copy with a highlighter is better than never running it by anybody but here is...

What To Look For In A 2nd Set of Eyes

You don't want people who are out to please you by saying "the copy is good" or "here is what I like about it".

You also don't want people who are trying to rewrite every sentence as if nothing you said is of value.

A great 2nd set of eyes will tell you when a paragraph is a little too long, confusing, or boring.

They will also find typos or places where you wrote something that seems to be the opposite of something written earlier.

If you have nobody else, join a Facebook group.

I wouldn't start tossing out a lot of work in a big copywriting group because you can damage your reputation when too many professionals see sloppy first and second drafts but there are a lot of smaller groups where the members would be happy to tell you what's wrong with your copy.

HOT TIP: If you are on Facebook, join The Gary Halbert Copy Club to find other copywriters who are always helping other wordsmiths.

https://www.facebook.com/groups/garyhalbertcopyclub/

Tip #5 Edit on Paper

Editing on a screen is just not as effective as editing on paper.

You can apply a lot of the steps in the editing formula on the computer but after a point, it's just easier to focus and catch more errors reading a printed copy so your last few edits should be done on paper.

With those 5 basic tips out of the way, here is some good advice.

When To Break The Rules of Grammar

Never confuse good grammar with good copywriting.

"Got Milk?" is a brilliant marketing campaign using bad grammar.

Don't sweat being grammatically correct until you are editing and even then you need to know when to break the rules.

Everyone eventually sends out copy with errors so it is helpful to know a good grammar Nazi and thankfully they are a dime a dozen.

It's easy to find someone who did really well in English class and LOVES to correct people and... the more money you get paid for writing, the more the grammarians love to point out your mistakes.

Use their ego to your advantage but don't forget to appear ashamed because it makes them feel better.

The grammar Nazis will relish another opportunity to feel superior later but don't shoot for absolute perfection.

It drives my favorite editor nuts but I myself choose not to use the Oxford Comma (the last comma before the word "and" in a list of words).

There is no official consensus on whether it is improper to not use an Oxford Comma and whenever I read one it gives me a slight pause which interrupts my flow for a microsecond so I choose not to use them.

I know top copywriters who do and don't use Oxford Commas and I have yet to see a test that shows they affect sales one way or the other.

The reason I choose not to use them is my goal is to write like I'm sitting in the room talking to you and I wouldn't put a pause right before saying "and".

When it comes to using words that don't exist like "moolah" or breaking up a sentence in the middle, forget the rules.

It's more important that the copy grips the reader and they only stop reading when they are frothing at the mouth to buy.

To do this we should now discuss...

How To Help Readers <u>Decide</u> To Read Your Copy

Section Two

How To Help Customers
Decide To Dive In To Your Copy

This section will give you tips designed to help customers decide to start reading your copy.

The idea behind the first part of the Halbert Editing Method is very simple.

Good Writing Creates Effortless Reading!

A lot of foolish marketers make the mistake of <u>not</u> thinking about their readers' state of mind <u>when</u> they are most likely to get the sales message and this error has put millions of dollars in the pockets of copywriters who take the time understand what prospects think and feel when they will be reading the copy.

For example ,we all check our email but we are in a different state of mind when we do.

Early in the morning when prospects check their email in-box on a workday, they are just trying to get a handle on their day and looking for what they *need* to deal with so... they sift through the emails with their fingers on the delete button.

Later, they may be checking their emails on a lunch break and have more time to read something which interests them.

On a Sunday these same people check their email looking for something interesting.

In direct mail, we always try to have business related offers show up on a Tuesday because the prospect is usually over the Monday rush and feels they have a handle on their workload and their minds aren't thinking about the weekend yet.

If the offer is for an entertaining event, you may want the message to come later in the week when the buyers are thinking about being off work but before they have committed to their weekend plans.

Even writers who think about when and where their readers will be when they get the copy, forget that once the reader glances at the copy...

The Prospect Must Choose To Start Reading!

After being hooked by the headline, a lot of writers assume the prospects will start reading the copy but this isn't necessarily true.

During the editing phase, your first job is to help the reader *decide* to start reading the copy and here is the problem.

People read ads and websites looking for value. They want to feel like they understand what may be important to them and move along very quickly.

In other words everyone is looking to feel completely informed and...

Once Readers Think They Know All They Need To Know They Start Looking For A Good Place To Stop Reading

Even with novels, the readers look for a good place to take a break from reading.

Don't Give It To Them!

When we get into advanced techniques, I'll show you how to force your prospects to read every damn word but let's start with making it easier for them to make that choice to start reading.

It all starts with...

Making The Copy Look Easy To Check Out

The number of people who read for entertainment has dropped significantly since I was a kid because the great bulk of society has replaced reading with watching videos and now most people only read out of necessity.

We also now demand information like news and learning to be delivered in bite size chunks and both of these facts indicate the attention span of the average American consumer is getting shorter and shorter.

In the old days of print advertising, there was only so much room you could afford and promotions were too expensive to get long winded, but not anymore.

I see a lot of super long-winded sales copy because someone told the copywriter that long copy sells better which is only sort of true.

Newbie copywriters use templates and extend all their selling points into 60 pages of copy regardless of how repetitive, irrelevant or boring the copy becomes.

In reality a lot of people stop reading when they get bored which happens faster and faster these days.

My brother put it best when he said, "write as if your prospect has to pee."

I take every opportunity to shorten copy that doesn't add to the power of the copy.

I go so far as to change "it is" to it's" but...

Brevity Doesn't Mean Write Short Copy

A lot of time has been spent debating long vs. short copy and the obvious answer is to test short and long versions of each campaign but that is not the kind of brevity I'm speaking of.

I'm just saying don't be long winded. Long copy can work great as long as you are quickly moving from one exciting statement to another but don't take forever getting to the point.

It's better to restate the same benefit three times than is to drag out getting to that selling point.

With that said, let's cover how to make your copy appear easy to check out.

Provide Eye Relief

After becoming attracted by a headline, readers are always assessing if it's worth taking the time to watch a video or start reading an email or newspaper.

The first step is to format copy so readers don't rule out reading the rest because it looks like heavy reading.

If the copy is one huge page-long paragraph, the reader will immediately sigh and weigh the decision to read even a little bit of the copy because nobody feels comfortable stopping in the middle of a paragraph.

However, if your promotion is made up of short, easy to read paragraphs and snippets of copy, the prospects are more likely to at least skim the copy or decide to start reading just a little to see if they want to read the rest.

My father called it Eye Relief and without it, you will lose everyone who doesn't have OCD.

Newbie writers think if the copy is interesting enough, people will read it. Wrong!

People get this notion because loved ones read their long copy and tell the author it was great.

The author just doesn't realize that everyone who didn't feel obligated to read the copy said, "Screw that, I have better things to do."

To really hammer this point home, on the next page is the introduction to this book without any formatting at all.

Intro **Do NOT Read!**

Before I share my proprietary and magic formula for editing copy, I want you to know two things. First, what I'm going to share with you will give you an advantage over even the best copywriters on earth but... it only helps make your message more readable, engaging and exciting. This formula can NOT make Eskimos want more ice. All the power in your sales copy comes from what you are saying and knowing your audience... not *how* you say it. In other words... market research is much more important than any creative writing ability. It takes marketing talent/experience to develop highly effective hooks, offers, and solutions from your research and the editing process which I'm going to thoroughly explain... is where all the professionalism comes into play. Just remember... no amount of clarity will make a bad offer better. Selling the wrong products to the wrong people at the wrong time will result in more wasted energy and resources than poorly worded copy. With that being said, this editing formula will definitely help make anything and everything you write from here on in, much smoother. The second thing I want you to know is... Why This Editing Formula Is So Valuable Reason One Few people know how to edit for sales copy. Schools mostly teach people how to write reports which are designed to pass on information to people forced to read it. Students are taught to state a premise, offer 3-5 supporting arguments and sum everything up into a nice package of information. Plus, college graduates have been taught to write 50 pages on something which only requires 5 pages and they are taught to boil down a whole philosophy into a one-page essay. Nobody is taught how to be entertaining or keep people interested in what's being said. Even in journalism, the articles are designed in such a way few people finish them because they give all the details you want to know up front and only

That was an extreme example which shows you how much our decision to read is affected by formatting.

The very first step in copy editing is to...

Break Up Your Copy Into Small Paragraphs

Your paragraphs should be no longer than 3-5 sentences.

Don't be afraid of the one sentence paragraphs either.

Novelists surely aren't.

Also, forget the rules of paragraphs you learned in school. Break up the paragraphs in any way that sounds natural.

Remember, the goal here is to make sure the copy looks easy to read so the prospects will decide to give the first few paragraphs a shot.

Don't put too much effort into where you are breaking up long paragraphs at this stage. I'll give you some tricks to breaking up paragraphs in a way which will help keep prospects reading later on in the formula.

At first you just want to break up paragraphs to make it easier on yourself to start editing.

The next step of breaking up sentences seems simple enough but I'll show you a way to turn those longer sentences into more powerful shorter statements.

Break Up Long Sentences

To break up sentences, my favorite technique is to hunt down the instances I have used the word "and" because most often I can take one long sentence and turn it into two shorter and more powerful statements.

For example...

Before:

This magic editing formula will make your copy smooth and after you use it you will be able to raise your rates.

After:

This magic editing formula will make your copy smooth.

After you use it you will be able to raise your rates.

Once you have broken your copy into easy to read paragraphs and shorter sentences it's time to move onto the next steps.

Punctuation Tips

A huge difference between writing for sales and all other forms of writing is good copy usually reads and feels more like a personal note than any formal type of written message.

One way to destroy the personal feel of a sales message is to give it a formal punctuation you would never expect in a note from a friend.

Here again I'm going to suggest you not worry as much about the rules of grammar as much as you should about getting your message across in a smooth way.

Let's take a look at some of the ways punctuation is used differently in sales copy compared to all other forms of writing.

Let's start with an example which highlights this concept perfectly.

The exclamation mark!

Rarely will anyone use more than one exclamation mark in any formal writing.

Even novels avoid using multiple exclamation marks like these!!!!!!!!!!!!!!

Yet if a co-worker gets upset about someone stealing their afternoon snack they may write STOP TAKING MY FOOD!!!!!!!!!!!!!!!

I'll cover when to use all capitalization later but all caps are also something more common in sales copy than in formal writing.

Commas- Insert commas whenever you would normally have a slight pause in your voice or take a natural breath when reading your copy out loud.

Normally, writers use commas, **like the commas to the left and right of this bold part of this sentence,** to highlight an explanation inside a sentence.

But normally the flow will be much smoother for the reader it you use parenthesis **(like the parenthesis to the left and right of this bold bold part of this sentence)** before moving back to the main point.

Never use semicolons like this ; They only disrupt the flow because your average reader has no idea why or when someone should use them and you don't want prospects to stop and think about the semicolon. I know many people will argue this point but this is my opinion and I'm sticking to it.

When To Indent Paragraphs

Indenting (adding a couple blank spaces at the beginning of every paragraph) provides extra eye-relief but it can sometimes throw off formatting.

If the copy is to be read in an image, a space ad, a magazine or any place where the printing will not change from viewer to viewer, you want to indent paragraphs and you may even want to leave one extra space between sentences.

If the indents can throw off the formatting because like when a viewer can control the print size you don't want to use them.

For example if you are reading the printed version of this little black book of editing secrets, you can see the beginning of every paragraph is indented but...

If you are reading this on a Kindle, Nook or other device which allows you to increase or decrease the font size, there are no indents because that would throw off the formatting if you size the copy too big.

This is one of several reasons pdf and using pictures of writing is so popular. You can still use indents because the extra spaces will be sized up or down with the rest of the copy in a way which will not throw off the reader.

Indenting paragraphs and adding an extra space between sentences may seem old fashioned but this will make your copy appear easier to read.

There are some very special formatting techniques for videos and web copy covered in the section on advanced techniques because they are usually taken care of by someone with a lot of technical skills but they do make digital copy and VSLs (Video Sales Letters) much more effective.

Fonts, Backgrounds and Line Spacing

Fonts and backgrounds are usually handled by someone in charge of design but as a copywriter you need to insist on two things.

1. The font must be easy to read.

Online I prefer to use Arial for a font and in print I like Courier New or Times New Roman because they are easy to read and nobody stops to think about how cool the font looks.

There are many other great choices which will work just fine but you don't ever want prospects to stop and think about how lovely your layout and design are.

Good copy is all about the message.

I know some marketers with degrees in graphic design will disagree to justify the time they spent in college but the fact is nobody remembers the fonts used in great promotions like the "Got Milk?" or "Just Do It!". What's remembered in effective campaigns is the message.

I'm not saying you shouldn't let the designers do their thing but make sure they don't screw up the message by making anyone stop to think about the font.

This is why I personally like the Times New Roman font. It is the default font in the most common word processing programs and used in so many books that it never stands out as out of the ordinary.

Anyway, just use common sense and read the copy to make sure the letter "t" doesn't look like the number 4 which I have seen.

2. You must insist on a background with a soft yet high contrast to the font. Black backgrounds with yellow or red fonts hurt your eyes very quickly.

Again, readability should trump all design concerns.

In print ads font size and line spacing are often dictated by how much copy is in your promotion and how much space you have to work with.

For long copy advertorial promotions you want to come close to matching the font, the font size and line spacing of the newspaper or magazine you are running your ad in.

No matter what, you should choose a font size and line spacing which makes the copy look easy to read in the format the customers will get the sales message.

If your ad will run on a bus bench it must be readable from a car. If you expect a lot of people to read your copy on a smart phone make sure your font isn't too big for an average size screen.

Always read your ad several times in the exact same situation your prospects will and make sure skimming and reading the copy is easy.

Inserting Subheads

Everyone who reads your copy will first become attracted by your headline or a picture but then all the readers can be divided into three distinct groups.

The first group of readers will start reading at the very beginning and read every word until they become bored or feel informed enough to move on without missing anything important.

The second group of readers will skim the copy and start reading right after the subheads or bullets they find attractive and continue reading until the end.

The third group of people will skim the ad very quickly trying to decide if they want to start reading the copy from the beginning and...

A Subhead Like This
Can Suck Undecided Readers
Into The Copy By Highlighting A Benefit
Not Covered In The Headline

Plus...

Subheads Also
Provide Eye Relief!

This works in space ads, webpage copy, direct mail campaigns and anywhere the prospect will be reading the copy so it is important to choose your subheads wisely.

When I teach marketing research, I show copywriters how to take all the features of a product or service and turn them into a long list of selling points and benefits to the buyers.

You want to take your list of benefits not mentioned in the headline and rank them by how important they are to buyers.

If you have the budget and the project has the potential for a big payoff you should survey real buyers and find out the best way to rank the benefits but that is a subject for marketing research.

Moving on.

Here are just a few of the benefits for this book about editing copy.

- Can Be Learned In One Afternoon

- Taken From The Patterns Found In The Best Promotions

- New Copywriting Lessons Never Heard Before

- Applying The Formula Gets Faster and Faster The More You Use It

- Works With Any And All Copy

- 40 Years of Copy Knowledge Boiled Down Into Simple Step-By-Step Instructions

- First Time Anyone Has Covered Editing Copy In Depth

- A Book Top Copywriter's Have Been Dying To Get Their Hands On

- Makes Your Copy Sound So Smooth You Can Raise Your Prices

- Explains How To Inject Hidden Psychology To Drive Sales Up

Any one of these benefits could be attractive to some potential buyers who are not excited by other benefits.

A veteran copywriter may not be worried about sounding like a veteran copywriter and some new copywriters may not have heard about Gary Halbert so I'll start with the most powerful benefit which applies to the most potential buyers.

In this case I think the most appealing benefit is the ability to raise copywriting fees.

- Makes Your Copy Sound So Smooth You Can Raise Your Prices

Now I want to massage the copy to make it shorter so it has more impact like this.

Works So Well You Can Raise Your Fee

I can explain why it works so well once I sucked them into the copy so I'd shorten it even further to say.

Raise Your Fee!

I can do this with all the benefits.

Injects Hidden Psychology

Proven To Drive Sales Up

Takes One Afternoon

**From The Patterns Used
In The Best Promotions**

**Brand New
Copywriting Lessons**

Gets Faster & Faster

Works On Any & All Copy

**40 Years of Proven
Copy Techniques**

**Step-By-Step
Instructions**

**Finally Copy Editing
Covered In Depth**

Now someone not 100% convinced they might miss out on something which could improve their lives if they don't read the copy may decide to read more because of one of these subheads.

I teach how to order your subheads and bullets in marketing research but once you have your first draft these subheads should be inserted right before you would explain or prove you can really provide these benefits.

In the section of this book about making the copy flow, I'm going to show you how to rework the copy just before and right after the subheads so the prospect reading the promotion from the beginning, and the prospect who starts reading right after the subhead can *both* continue reading without missing a beat.

Section Three
Editing For Clarity

This section will explain how you can polish your first draft until the reader falls through the copy without skipping a beat.

This is the first step in creating what copywriters call the greased slide effect because if done right, the reader will forget they are reading until they have an uncontrollable urge to buy.

This simple trick will help you spot errors even professional editors miss.

Read Your Copy Out Loud!

Don't make the mistake of thinking you will spot where the writing doesn't flow by silently rereading what you wrote.

It just isn't the same as reading the copy out loud and I'm going to prove it to you.

When we reread our own words silently to ourselves, we skip over hiccups in the flow and keep on reading because we are really only looking for grammatical errors.

If you read the same piece of copy aloud, it becomes impossible not to find where the copy no longer flows and...

Copy flow is super important because I never want the prospect to even think about the fact that they are reading. I want to give them every one of their thoughts. If they have to reread even one word, I have failed to control their every thought and it breaks the spell I want them under.

If embarrassment stops you from reading aloud, do it while you are alone or tell people near you it is an old Gary Halbert trick for better writing.

To really prove this point, I have taken a writing sample from the website www.ezinearticles.com

To be perfectly clear, this article was chosen as a writing sample because it has all the elements of decent copy.

It was written by a professional and then edited by another professional but... this helps me prove that all good copy can still flow better using the Halbert formula for editing.

Now I'm not critiquing this article or disparaging the work in any way.

Enhancing the flow of my own copy just wouldn't prove my point nearly as well as improving the copy of another professional writer.

Below is the article as it was published. Read it silently once and then read it again out loud.

All entrepreneurs know just how hard it is to run your own business. In today's highly competitive marketplace, you are faced with the daily challenges that threaten to steal your customers and squeeze your profits.

Practically every business I have ever consulted is guilty of making some of the ten worst marketing mistakes. While there are a number of critical marketing strategies that every successful business owner can use to insure success, there are ten that are the most important.

Some are very serious and must be corrected immediately or will cause dangerous consequences for your business. I want to share three of them with you right now. By eliminating these errors from your business, you can literally leapfrog your competitors and dramatically impact your sales and profits.

Mistake 1. NOT HAVING A STRATEGIC MARKETING POSITION AND ARTICULATING IT CLEARLY

A SMP is the critical sales message that you project to your customers and prospective customers that tells them very concisely:

1) Who you are and what it is that makes your business special and unique.

2) What benefit or result they will get if they do business with you over one of your competitors.

3) What your guarantee or customer satisfaction policy is.

Again, this author is good, but copy can always be improved which is why we are trying to improve something already well written.

It might encourage you to know my own writing needs to be reworked a couple of times to look as good as our sample here.

Below is the same article, except I've underlined the places where there is a break in the flow.

All entrepreneurs know just how hard it is to run your own business. In today's highly competitive marketplace, you are faced with the daily challenges that threaten to steal your customers and squeeze your profits. Practically every business I have ever consulted is guilty of making some of the ten worst marketing mistakes. While there are a number of critical marketing strategies that every successful business owner can use to insure success, there are ten that are the most important.

Some are very serious and must be corrected immediately or will cause dangerous consequences for your business. I want to share three of them with you right now. By eliminating these errors from your business, you can literally leapfrog your competitors and dramatically impact your sales and profits.

Mistake 1. NOT HAVING A STRATEGIC MARKETING POSITION AND ARTICULATING IT CLEARLY

A SMP is the critical sales message that you project to your customers and prospective customers that tells them very concisely:

1) Who you are and what it is that makes your business special and unique.
2) What benefit or result they will get if they do business with you over one of your competitors.
3) What your guarantee or customer satisfaction policy is.

There are at least five spots where the flow was not very smooth. These were not easy to spot unless you read the copy out loud.

We will discuss how to repair some of those hiccups throughout the rest of the formula but you can simply start by rephrasing anything which doesn't sound smooth.

Pronoun Hunt

As I said before, you don't want anything to interrupt your flow during the copy dump and it's only natural that while getting caught up in storytelling and making offers you will use a lot of pronouns like "he", "she", "it", "they", or "them".

These are called pronouns which is any word that takes the place of the formal name of anything so the list of pronouns is huge. For example let's suppose my next line was... "when it comes to pronouns, let's start looking for the most important one."

In this instance the word "one" is used as a pronoun. Which I'll fix in a moment.

The problem is the copy is always clear in the author's head but it's easy for the reader to lose track of who or what the pronouns are referring to.

Ever get lost as someone tells you a story about multiple people using too many pronouns like "he" and "him or "she" and "her"?

It's even more of a problem in print or in a video than in person because you can't stop and ask the storyteller for clarity.

You can simply replace pronouns with the proper names the pronouns refer to but you can also use this next trick to punch up the copy.

When I teach copywriters how to do marketing research I make them write out a list of ways they want customers to describe the business, product, service, or subject of the copy.

Once the first draft is complete you can go back and replace those pronouns with these better descriptions without sounding too repetitive.

Here is an example.

Let's suppose I was writing an article about my father.

Now on my list of descriptions of my father I have put Legendary Marketer, Top Copywriter, Prince of Print, Master Wordsmith and the list goes on.

So after writing about my dad I may have to replace the words he or him but I can use far better descriptions than just "dad" or "Gary."

I can say "I took all the patterns I saw in the work of The World's Greatest Copywriter and put them into a simple step-by-step editing formula anyone can use to write copy so smooth they sound like The Prince of Print.

Almost every time you see the words I, He, She, They, Them or It, you can replace them with far more powerful descriptions in the list we just made.

Question the use of each pronoun you find.

Here is another example. Earlier I wrote:

"Let's start with the most important one."

This becomes much more clearer if we drop the word "one" and spell out what we are talking about.

Now it reads:

Let's start with the most important pronoun to hunt down.

Again you just need to question each one and if the copy would be more clear if you spelled out what the pronoun refers to do so. Or consider if your sentence would still be clear if you removed the word.

Perform A "THAT" Hunt

Basically, all writers use the word "that" too often in writing.

We use it as a crutch to stitch together clauses. In almost every instance, the writing will flow better, read more professionally and have more impact when we remove what my father called the superfluous "that"s.

About 90% of the time, it's best to eliminate or replace the word "that" but don't go too nuts.

Remember the goal is not to eliminate ALL of them. Roughly 10% of the time you need to use the "that".

Okay let me show you how this works.

Every time you come across the word "that" used in a sentence, try reading that sentence aloud without the word 'that' or try replacing the word 'that' with the word 'which'.

If either sounds better make the change.

Here are some examples from some copy about a webinar I held.

Simple Elimination of the word "that"

Good: During the webinar we'll explain the trick that every professional overlooked.

Better: During the webinar we'll explain the trick every professional overlooked.

Replacement of the word 'that"

Good: This is the brilliant trick that got Amazon to send out emails every month promoting The Boron Letters for me.

Better: This is the brilliant trick which got Amazon to send out emails every month promoting The Boron Letters for me.

To punch up the copy I rearranged these sentences to eliminate the need for using the words "that" or "which".

Best: The webinar reveals the simple trick every other professional Amazon publisher overlooks.

This brilliant strategy got Amazon to send out emails each and every month promoting The Boron Letters.

As you can see the polished and edited version can look quite different from the raw copy so keep that in mind when pouring everything into your first draft.

Big Word Hunting

You never want to talk above your audience for a lot of reasons.

The most important reason is you never want to write anything that would stop the reader from letting you control their mind.

I was taught you don't want readers to think about your writing skill or anything other than your message.

Nobody should have to reread sentences to make sure they understand them and...

It's not all about IQ. No matter how extensive your vocabulary is, nobody memorizes the dictionary. The minute you read a word you are not familiar with your mind is no longer being sucked into the copy.

Good wordsmiths create or have a natural rhythm and they make the copy so simple the reader falls through it in a trance of increasing excitement.

Using big or unfamiliar words can break that spell.

My father had his vocabulary tested in Boron and his scores were off the charts but you would never know it reading his work or speaking to him.

He took me on reading vacations. We would hit up a library and bookstores before heading to Santa Barbara or Palm Springs where we would check into a hotel and just read all weekend.

He knew the meaning of every word I ever asked him about but nobody would ever say his propensity for prolixity placed him on the precipice of pomposity because he was first and foremost a persuader and it's easier to get what you want from people who like you because you don't make them feel uneducated or stupid.

Making the reader feel like they may not always understand you is terrible for good communication or trust building.

Hunt down the big words and replace them with more simple and common words.

There are computer programs (some free) which find and highlight big words. These programs can also tell you what grade-level your copy is written at so we listed one in the resources section at the back of this book.

Print advertising in newspapers should shoot for writing at or below the 6th grade level.

The lower, the better.

It's always great to have a measuring tool but don't sweat what the program says too much.

In fact, I have never used it because by following this editing formula I am already shortening sentences and I work really hard to make everything super clear.

My buddy Scott Haines (great copywriter) was curious and put an email sales letter I wrote through just such a program which told him it was written at the 3.5 grade level.

Some of my father's copy is written at the 3rd grade reading level and he certainly never laid eyes on a program which measured the readability of his copy.

This proves you can simplify copy using common sense alone but...

It's easier to improve things you measure and I highly recommend using the writing programs listed in the resources section.

Again I wouldn't bend over backwards shooting to write at the 3rd grade level but the programs can point out a lot of opportunities to simplify your copy.

When you do find words you may want to break out a thesaurus to find a simpler alternative to replace them with.

Actually it's funny. In college they teach you to pull a thesaurus out to find bigger words but when writing for sales, you want to swap big words for little ones.

Repeat Word Hunting

As I said earlier, you want the reader or viewer to be so wrapped up in the message that they let your copy take over and do all the thinking for them.

When words are repeated too often it can jar readers or viewers back into their own reality.

If you watch well scripted TV show, movies or video sales letters, you will notice they don't like to use the same words close together.

When I write about my father, I switch back and forth between using the word father, dad, and pop.

Overuse of one word gets annoying quickly and it's an easy fix.

Almost every word in the English language has a perfectly good and simple substitute you can find in a thesaurus.

Another tip I got from John Carlton is to not use the same verb twice in a single page.

Insert Transitions

Once your copy has been edited several times and the elements like story, benefits, bullets and so on are all in the final order... you want to use transitions and cliffhangers when it is needed to smooth out the rough spots.

This is usually where the copy abruptly jumps from one point to an unrelated point.

In these cases, it is handy to use transitions. Here is an example...

Before

> The handwritten version of The Boron Letters is raw and uncensored!
>
> I'll be signing and numbering the first batch to come off the presses and embossing each with the old corporate seal for Cherrywood Publishing.

After

> The handwritten version of The Boron Letters is raw and uncensored!
>
> Anyway, I'll be signing and numbering the first batch to come off the presses and embossing each with the old corporate seal for The Gary Halbert Letter.

Here are some more examples of transitions...

Moving on...

Anyway,

However,

Also,

Plus,

You can use these transitions to start the next sentence or in the case of "Moving on..." you can use it in between paragraphs.

Section Four

How To Keep The Prospect Reading

This section will show you several (classic and some never before shared) tricks to make a reader feel like they can't stop reading or without missing out on something which will improve their life.

Setting A Hook or Anchor

I don't always use this very effective technique. Especially if I can keep saying more and more exciting things to the prospect which will keep them wanting more.

Also, what I'm about to explain is not really an editing trick but I must still mention it because this technique is usually put into the first draft to keep the prospect reading.

A lot of copywriters call this a takeaway but I don't like that term because the term takeaway also refers to qualifying the prospect which is when you write about who should not respond to the ad so it can get confusing. I prefer the term anchor.

Basically what you want to do is promise the reader they will get some exciting information if they continue reading the copy. You then put off delivering on that promise until they have already been sucked in to your sales pitch.

For example you may say something like, "In a moment I'm going to reveal how to get the primary email address of everyone who signs up for your email list but first I need to explain how and why this adds up to thousands of extra dollars to your profit."

This promise to give them something of value as a reward for reading your copy goes a long way to keeping the prospect reading but again this is not part of the editing process because what you promise to give them usually depends heavily upon your research and the hook you have chosen for your headline.

One classic example was my father's ad with the headline...

The Amazing Secret of The Marketing Genius Who is Afraid To Fly

Truth be told he never even delivered on the promise of explaining his "Amazing Secret" but by the time the true prospects finished reading the ad they didn't notice and all they wanted to do was hire the marketing genius who was Jay Abraham.

Now with that out of the way let's get on with editing tricks designed to keep the prospects reading.

Earlier I explained that most people reading or viewing promotions are looking for a place to stop reading knowing they won't be missing anything important to their life.

In other words they will continue reading if they think there might be information coming up which will make their life better or they should know to avoid problems.

I also explained that the best strategy is to never give them a place to feel safe if they stop reading and here's how to do that.

Let's start with cliffhangers.

Cliffhangers

The subtle nuances of when and how to use transition phrases and cliffhangers separates the pros from amateurs but it's not too difficult if you know what to do.

You don't want to overuse transitions phrases or make every sentence end on a cliffhanger.

Cliffhangers take the most skill.

It's way too easy to get cheesy by using too many tired old lines like "but wait there's more."

The best way to get people to jump from one paragraph to another is to break up whole paragraphs where one thought naturally leads to the other as I already described.

I also explained how breaking up sentences can lead to great cliffhangers and how to use the magical ellipsis.

We also covered a few transition phrases. You want a nice mix of all of these before you insert any cliffhangers.

The point is...

Make readers feel like they are getting good info and there is no really good place to stop reading without feeling they were about to get even more good info and... falling from one easy-to-read line to the next.

You want the reader so caught up in the copy they forget about everything going on around them and too many cliffhangers, incomplete thoughts, or transitions will break that spell.

Always aim for a nice mix which is hardly noticeable.

Keep the words simple, the stories exciting, the paragraphs small, the copy smooth, and the message exciting.

As a last resort you can insert cliffhangers.

Add a clause to the previous line hinting at what they will know next.

For example:

Original Copy:

> The two day intensive marketing research workshop is only $4,997
>
> You only have to learn one or two new tricks like how to find your customers, the best way to know when your future customers are eager to buy, or how to sound like one of your prospects to build trust.
>
> Any of these can make a promotion go from dying to thriving.
>
> If I'm wrong, you will have had a tax free weekend with colleagues and a Halbert certification but...
>
> What if I'm right?
>
> If I am right, you will make your money back in spades on the very next successful promotion.

Edited Copy With Mix of Cliffhangers and Other Transitions Added:

> The two day intensive marketing research workshop is $4,997 and here is why that is ridiculously cheap.
>
> You only have to learn one or two new tricks like how to find your customers or the best way to know when your future customers are eager to buy or how to sound like one of your prospects to build trust because...
>
> Any of these can make a promotion go from dying to thriving.
>
> If I'm wrong, you will have had a tax free weekend with colleagues and a Halbert certification but...
>
> What if I'm right?
>
> If I am right, you will make your money back in spades on the very next successful promotion.

Yes, I am that picky about how I end a sentence and all good wordsmiths are.

How picky usually depends upon deadlines and the promotion's potential payoff but in the best of the best sales copy, every word has earned its place.

Another great cliffhanger technique is to simply sum up what you said before and then give the reader only half of the next point.

For example I could add..

> And now that you know the marketing research workshop is guaranteed to boost your skills or you get your money back, let me explain why you want to drop everything and attend.

More Cliffhangers

Here are a few cliffhangers you can use to end a sentence...

..and things got worse/better.

then came the shocking part.

but boy am I glad I did/didn't

that I now regret

The Simplest Cliffhanger Trick of All

One of the easiest cliffhangers to use is to simply end the sentence with the word "but" or "so" and then add ellipse but...

Don't overdo it or the reader will get annoyed.

In fact I don't like to use the word "but" too often because it sounds like an argument so...

If I feel I have used the word "but" too often I will replace a few with the word "yet".

If the word "but" is in the middle of a sentence and can be replaced with the words "and" or "plus" I like that even better.

Complete Sentences With Incomplete Thoughts

Another way to make the reader feel like they must continue reading or they will be missing something is to use complete sentences which are basically incomplete thoughts.

Let's suppose your copy starts to tell your story which the prospect feels is very much like their story.

For example:

1. It took several weeks but I finally built an email list and then spent another week perfecting an email which I knew would be useful to everyone on my list.

2. I had a few friends review the email to be sure it was good and then sent it out at what I thought was the right time.

3. When the results came back I was devastated.

Each of these sentences is complete but the thoughts are not.

The first sentence begins to tell a story which is only the set up.

The second sentence leaves the reader unsure of where the story is going.

The third sentence tells you the result but leaves you wondering why.

The sentences may appear to be cleverly crafted but it's not hard to do the same thing with your own copy.

All you need to do is rearrange the sentences in your first draft.

Here is the next sentence before and after rearranging.

Before

Less than 25% of the list opened the email and there was a red alert from my email list management company warning me that several people had reported my email as spam.

After

1. Less then 25% of the list opened the email.

2. Even worse, there was a red alert from my email list management company.

3. Several people had reported my email as spam and I knew I had to find a better way.

As you can see, I broke up the last sentence into three separate statements which are all incomplete thoughts.

The difference between a cliffhanger and an incomplete sentence is subtle but very important.

A cliffhanger directly tells the reader what you are about to share such as "but that's not the worst part."

An incomplete thought leaves the reader wanting to know what happens next on their own or why.

For example, I read a headline which said a particular politician was unique in that he was hated by everyone on both sides of the aisle.

This just leaves people wanting to know why so they continue to read further.

Another way to put it is a cliffhanger says there is more to the story while an incomplete thought just leaves the story obviously incomplete.

A high note is when you write something which makes the prospect think, "oh that's a great idea" and then want more great ideas.

The reason the distinction is important is to keep the reader's... attention. You want a mix of cliffhangers, incomplete thoughts and high notes.

Too much of any one of these will irritate the reader and if blended nicely the reader won't notice the tactics and because of the high notes the prospect will feel like they are getting a lot out of the copy.

It's All About Rhythm

When it comes to sentence and paragraph length or cliffhangers, high points, and transitions it's all about rhythm which you can detect while reading out loud.

You will notice when reading a paragraph is so long you have to stop in the middle to catch your breath meaning it's too long.

You will also be able to spot when you have gone overboard by using too many cliffhangers.

A lot of copywriters are also good musicians and comedians. The reason is all three focus a lot on timing.

Comedians quickly learn to make sure the surprisingly funny part of their jokes come at the very end of what they say and musicians understand how a lack of rhythm becomes boring very quickly.

If your copy sounds like it has a natural rhythm which is flowing up and down when it's read out loud, you have it right.

Section Five

How To Punch Up Copy

This section focuses on ways to massage the copy while editing to boost sales.

How To Highlight Words

Once you have read your copy out loud a few times you can punch up the copy and add even more eye relief by formatting individual words and phrases.

When reading your copy out loud you will notice which words need extra emphasis.

In VSLs (Video Sales Letters) this will help you know when the presenter should change tone and pitch.

Now, in print there are all kinds of ways to emphasize words.

The following guide is only going to give you a rough idea of the way I view the power behind certain formatting.

There are no hard rules for when to use italics vs. underlining but I can give you a few pointers.

Copywriting is less about the art of writing than the art of communication.

When you have exciting news to share, how great the news is dictates how much emphasis you put on that news.

Bad news is usually delivered in a low hush voice. When the news is so freaking great you can barely contain yourself, you may even literally empty your lungs, shouting your message at the top of your voice.

When you read your copy aloud, it should sound like you are talking to someone in person and you should try to give readers the same level of emphasis in print as you would when speaking to them.

In other words you should only use **ALL BOLD CAPS WHEN THE NEWS IS FANFREAKINGTASTIC!!!!!!**

When you need just a little emphasis *italics* will work.

Here is the list of ways to highlight words and phrase in the order I think goes from least to most emphatic.

Italics
"Quotes"

<u>Underlining</u>
Bolding
ALL CAPS
<mark>Highlighting</mark>
High-Contrast Colors
Size Matters Too
Moving Text

You can of course mix these formats to make them even more emphatic so the options are endless.

For example, ALL CAPS is pretty damn emphatic but **ALL CAPS IN BOLD** is even stronger. **ADD IN EXCLAMATION MARKS LIKE THESE !!!!** and you can really start going crazy.

Just give everything what you feel is the appropriate amount of emphasis. The key is to not make every single word stand out nor to overuse any one way to emphasize.

It's like screaming. A raised voice does get attention but constantly yelling just annoys people.

When you realize this and when you are careful not to overdo it, you can use the most powerful print emphasis of all which is moving/flashing.

The secret to using moving or flashing text is to make it go away or stop all motion quickly.

Online, you should only place a blinking "SALE" sign somewhere the reader won't see for long or the flashing will become too distracting.

Inserting Power Words

Most of the top copywriting courses provide a list of power words including my father's but I think this is a mistake.

Using words like "crisis" instead of "problem" really goes a long way to punch up your copy and excite prospects which keeps them reading but... there is a serious flaw in using someone "else's" list of power words.

Personally I'm sick of the word "Amazing"... Sorry dad but after 30+ years it gets a little stale and that isn't my main objection to using a power word list from other copywriters.

You see, every wordsmith eventually settles into their own writing style and certain words just don't fit naturally.

Every time I see someone try to mimic John Carlton's dark Steven King-like way of writing it feels forced.

Here is a better way...

Go to The National Enquirer every day for a week or two and read a bunch of their headlines.

Pay attention to which words really grab you and use them to make two lists.

One list should be made up of positive words like "Miracle" and "Jaw-Dropping" and the other list should contain all of the negative words like "Slime Ball" and "Crisis".

This idea of using power words also applies to phrases you may like such as "River of income" or "Impossible to find" or "goes together like hookers and blow".

Okay I let that last one in just to show this also works for copywriters who like to take a more abrasive and attention jarring approach.

[NOTE:] You will find a lot more negative words than positive words but if you begin to keep your eyes and ears open for such power words, you will build both lists over time but here is the best part.

Eventually you will write using your attention gripping power words and refer to the list less and less but... you will always want to keep your list of power words handy when writing and editing because it can help keep the mental juices flowing.

What you want to do is read your list of power words and phrases right before writing your first draft and then refer to the list during the editing phase.

While editing you will swap out words like "upset" with "livid" or maybe change "rare" to "impossible to find".

Section Six

Injecting Hidden Psychology

This section focuses on psychological tricks which help a prospect's desire to buy.

Remove Qualifiers

When I write a first draft, I'm trying to get all of my thoughts down really fast and I end up leaving in a few qualifier words.

Qualifiers are the words that limit the power of other words, phrases, and claims.

Here are some examples of words that are qualifiers:

Like
Some
Mostly
Partially
Could
May
Possibly

Look out for these words and here is what to do when you find them.

First, I ask myself if the word makes the statement more accurate and if it does... I leave it.

You always want to say the best thing you can about offers but...

You want to be able to back up everything you write in a court of law and the court of public opinion.

That being said, qualifier words sneak into your first drafts <u>way</u> too often and qualifiers which really don't need to be there should be dropped like a bad habit.

For example, I once wrote... "The Gary Halbert Letters All-Star Audio Series contains some of the best copywriters on earth."

Now I could have legally said this because it is an opinion and "the best" is sort of subjective but...

I felt that there was one guy missing from the top tier of wordsmiths who would make me and a lot of others question if we really had all the <u>*very*</u> "best" writers.

In other words, I felt like saying we had the best copywriters simply wasn't 100% honest when I believed one of the gentlemen missing was better than one of the other writers in our top 5 list so the statement would not have been true without using the word "some".

As it turns out... the gentleman I felt was missing did come on board so we ended up with ALL of the top copywriters so I felt it was time to remove the word "some" and tell the world that...

The Gary Halbert Letter
All-Star Audio Series
Has <u>THE</u> Top Copywriters On Earth!

I'm not one of them and I'm not saying everyone in the series is in the top 20 but I can defend my statement both in a court of law and the court of public opinion so I'm now willing to make it because I don't believe anyone can say they are better than all the copywriters in that line up.

Qualifying words sound subtle when you write and read them but there is a big difference between "This may work" and "This WILL work!"

Adverb Hunt

This is one of those tips you don't want to follow so strictly you never use an adverb (words that modifies a verb or adjective such as very or absolutely).

Qualifiers are usually adverbs that attempt to limit the following statement like using the word "mostly" to basically say "not all" in this case we are looking for the words that are trying to emphasize the next word by saying things like "extremely" and just to make this clear, here is an example.

Let's suppose I am talking about this editing formula and I write...

"The steps outlined in this book are extremely effective in keeping your reader engaged."

This statement is more emphatic if I eliminate the adverb "extremely"

In fact many of the adverbs you should be looking out for end with the letters "LY".

Anyway, many copywriters feel such words show laziness to find an even more powerful description so instead of saying "the room is very messy" or "this technique is extremely effective" you might eliminate the adverbs and go with "the room looked like a hurricane came through" or "this is a powerful technique" but don't go too far with this.

Sometimes an adverb does help add punch so here is what you want to do in this step of the editing process.

When you find an adverb in your copy jot down a few alternative ways to say the same thing and then go with your gut as to which makes a stronger statement.

Sometimes the way you phrased something with an adverb is the best choice of words and sometimes you will find an even more powerful way to put something.

At first this may seem like over analyzing but the best of the best copywriters do just that. They fret about each and every word and this is how a rough draft becomes a masterpiece.

The "I" To "You" Formula

Great copywriters say it's best to personalize your promotions and write one on one communications while other well-respected wordsmiths tell you to never speak of yourself.

They are both half right.

Lots of people make money on nothing more than their ego but listening to someone talk about themselves gets boring super fast so here is how to strike a good balance.

It's simple enough to remove most instances where you talk about yourself but the goal is not to avoid speaking about yourself completely.

After all, a lot of the time you are sharing your story to explain your qualifications or build trust. So how do we do this without becoming really annoying?

The answer is very simple.

Here is my formula.

It's always okay to talk about yourself in a negative light. It is the *bragging* people get sick of fast so here is how you get the best of both worlds.

You talk about yourself in the negative and when the story turns positive you immediately make everything about the reader's benefit.

It's easy. When mentioning yourself, make sure your wins appear to be the result of good luck you recognize or explain that the greatness is the result of very hard tedious work which the reader can make quick use of for their own personal gain.

Here's an example...

"No matter how much time I spent writing, my copy never quite seemed to have that attention gripping edge until... I started studied copywriting masterpieces written by my father and put his editing process into a formula you can use to sound like Gary Halbert."

Again, you don't want to disrupt your flow while writing the first draft worrying about not mentioning yourself. If you fret about every little detail, before writing, you will never get any first draft going.

Always save ironing out such issues and punching up the copy for the editing phase.

Like the word "and" the words "but" and "yet" leads to a lot of opportunities to shorten sentences but...

Sometimes these words can be used to bait the reader with curiosity so they read the next sentence like I just did.

Here is another example:

A few paragraphs back, I wrote..

> "I'll cover rearranging sentences and when to break paragraphs in the section on advanced editing techniques but... right now, I just want you to find long sentences and break them up.

See how this breaks up nicely into two separate sentences.

> "I'll cover rearranging sentences and when to break paragraphs in the section on advanced editing techniques.
>
> Right now, I just want you to look for long sentences and break them up."

However... even further back I wrote:

"There are no hard rules for when to use italics vs. underlining but I can give you a few pointers."

Everything written after the word "but", is designed to make you feel the need to read the next sentence.

It's a complete sentence but an incomplete thought.

I already explained that most ad readers are looking for a place to stop reading without missing anything critical.

The key is to break up paragraphs and end sentences in a way which leaves the reader feeling incomplete if they don't read more.

When you do come to an exciting statement make sure it is at the end of the sentence.

Comedians know this better than anyone.

The surprise of the joke has to be the very last thing said and if you learn this one tactic you can really keep people reading.

Without a cliffhanger or incomplete thought, you are relying on the excitement of the last statement to get readers to bother looking at the next paragraph.

When I break up a paragraph by using ellipses, end the paragraph with with an incomplete thought or cliffhanger, or insert a transition, my #1 goal is to make the reader feel like they are missing something which may be in the next paragraph.

Whenever I have finally come to a complete point, I end it on such a high note the reader craves more.

Moving on...

Now it is time to share some of my own additions to my dad's formula.

First let's start hunting down all the uses of the word "I"

We really want to question our use of the word "I" because readers hate hearing people talk about themselves unless they are sharing negative news.

People love to read things like "I was beat up in jail and worried about survival" but they never want to read "I was cruising down the street in my Ferrari."

It is too easy to sound self-absorbed and put people off by talking about yourself. Try to avoid doing so.

Writers are often relating their own experiences or sharing their knowledge. Plus, good copywriters write to the reader in a personal way, so it is very natural for us to use the word I and drift into talking about ourselves.

Many times you can just remove the entire clause and the copy will be better. Sometimes it isn't so easy.

In our example one paragraph reads:

> Some are very serious and must be corrected immediately or will cause dangerous consequences for your business. ==I want to share three of them with you right now.== By eliminating these errors from your business, you can literally leapfrog your competitors and dramatically impact your sales and profits.

After removing the highlighted portion it is shorter which is good and it reads better

> Some are very serious and must be corrected immediately or will cause dangerous consequences for your business. By eliminating just three of these ten errors from your business, you can literally leapfrog your competitors and dramatically impact your sales and profits.

The copy still states the article only covers three of the ten mistakes.

However, you may have noticed we did not remove the instance where he mentioned he was a consultant. One of the points of writing this article is to show the world he is a professional.

Sometimes you have to speak about yourself to tell your story or to prove your credibility to the reader. Basically you have to sell yourself. Just don't do it when you don't have to.

When appropriate, change the word "I" to "We" or remove them altogether as WE have done in this article.

Another trick to cleaning up copy, is to break up long sentences when possible. Writers tend to feel sentences should be a certain length. However, to the reader, shorter is always better.

Sentences May Be Too Long, But Never Too Short!

We already used this trick with one of the sentences we reworked during our "that" hunt.

That Hunt Example

We changed:

> While there are a number of critical marketing strategies that every successful business owner can use to ensure success, there are ten that are the most important.

The new copy reads:
> There are a number of critical marketing strategies every successful business owner can use to ensure success. Ten of them are the most important.

How To Use Technical Jargon
To Build Trust & Authority

During your research, you should also have written down a lot industry specific technical words and jargon used by experts in the subject of your offer.

You should insert the technical words wherever appropriate and then quickly explain what they mean so the reader feels like you are a pro who won't confuse them. This helps establish trust and makes the reader comfortable.

For example when writing for the finance industry I may use the term PE Ratio which shows the reader I know what I am talking about but often they may not know what I am talking about so...

I then explain exactly what that means so the reader not only recognizes I am an authority but the reader also starts to trust that I won't leave them confused.

In this example I would write P/E Ratio which is just the price divided by earnings or what the company made in the last 3 months.

When you use words the prospects don't understand like technical jargon, the readers lose comfort which is hard to get back but nobody who matters will ever say "gee I like what you are saying but you didn't make it complicated enough."

Moving Answers To Questions & Objections

Once you have read your copy a few times you will start to see where and when a potential buyer may begin to have questions but you don't want to answer questions once the prospect has them.

You want to answer questions BEFORE future buyers can even think of them.

The way to do this is simple.

Let's suppose at one point in the copy it would be natural for the buyer to wonder what makes me an expert on a particular subject.

Let us also assume the answer to that question is over 40 years of real world experience.

All you have to do is mention the 40 years of real world experience just before the point where a serious buyer would have that question.

For example, if I was writing copy to sell a book on editing sales copy and I think the point a wordsmith might wonder what makes me an expert is right after they learn I wrote such a book, I would say something like this:

"I have taken all the patterns I learned spending over 40 years reading, testing, making money, and writing my own money-making copy from my father, the legendary copywriter Gary Halbert and put it all into a book."

Now you know my credentials before you even know about the book.

Let's suppose you know their objection will be 32 steps sounds like a formula which will take a lot of time to implement.

I will then say something such as...

"The best part is, once you know the formula it will begin to seep into your writing and you will be able to apply more and more of these secret tactics every time you edit.

In fact, soon you will be using all 32 parts of the magic editing process in just one or two passes."

Again I have addressed the potential objection just before the prospect gets enough information to become concerned.

It won't take much practice before you will know your Iron Clad 100% Satisfaction or You Get Your Money Back guarantee comes before the price or you have to explain your solution is simple before they can think it sounds complicated.

The "So What" Test

Here is a little copy related story you will dig.

Another copywriter and I both wrote completely separate promotions for the exact same product mailed to the exact same list but instead of running a simple split test we did something a little special.

He let me edit his copy and run that too.

The results helped me prove a big point.

You see my copy and the version of the other writer's copy I edited both outperformed the other wordsmith's original copy 4 to 1. This means for every sale that copy took in each of the other two pieces of edited copy took in 4.

Now since my own copy and the copy I edited roughly pulled in the same number of sales, it proved the losing copy had great selling points and covered enough features and benefits to sell as well as my version.

So what made the difference?

The difference was I performed the "so what" test.

All I did was read the other writer's copy pretending I was a super busy, self-centered and stuck up prick and I then cut out everything that sounded boring or made me feel like saying, "yeah, so what?"

This is easier than it sounds and it's fun.

Take for example the following paragraphs.

Hi,

My name is Bond Halbert and I have a degree in International Business Administration with a minor in economics.

Last Summer, my wife and I took a vacation with my kids to Italy and that's where I had a great idea.

You see, my son was sick and I chose to stay behind in the hotel to be with him while my wife and daughter went sightseeing.

Anyway, while there, I decided to get some work done but I realized, I left my copywriting reference library back in the states.

What did I do?

Well, I went to Amazon to look for the books I knew I needed and I made an amazing discovery.

There are absolutely no books on how to edit copy.

For years, I have helped a lot of professionals clean up copy so I decided to write a book on...

How To Force Potential Customers To Read Every Single Word You Write!

That copy was so boring I almost fell asleep writing it and it's about me.

Let's take a look after I ruthlessly cut out everything a self-centered and very busy potential buyer would NOT care about.

The subhead may tease them into reading the copy but the copy has no kick and I doubt I would look forward to reading more.

Hi,

My name is Bond Halbert and for years, I have helped a lot of professionals clean up copy so I wrote a new book titled ...

How To Force Potential Customers

To read

Every Single Word You Write!

Notice, I even chopped out the word "decided" because nobody cares why or how I decided to write a book.

When it comes time to reassuring buyers my editing formula won't make them look bad, it might be helpful to mention my Bachelor's Degree in Int'l Business Administration but it's way down on the list of my credentials when it comes to editing.

Stories that build trust and statements to prove credibility need to come at the right time in the copy which is right before someone would naturally wonder about them.

I'll cover how to do this later in this book.

Change Words People Secretly Hate

Great copywriters understand people. They know what people really think vs. what they say because they are brutally honest about themselves.

For example I don't want to learn guitar, I want to be able to play guitar.

You know what I like more than earning money? I like being given money and if I have to make money I want to make *easy* money.

People want to be recognized for their work but they don't want to work.

We humans prefer simple tricks to learning professional techniques and we would rather have a quick fix than a plan of attack.

When editing your copy be sure to look for words people secretly avoid.

For example I don't use words like "teach" or "learn" because that sounds hard.

Instead, I replace those words with statements like "once I show you this simple trick you will know the secret too".

I once saw a headline which promised to teach me to be a leader in my community and thought leadership sounds like responsibility and work. Screw that.

Once you start looking for words which trigger a feeling you would like to avoid it's easy to replace them with an endless amount of alternatives.

You can replace "teach you how" with "give you the formula", "let you in on the secret" or "hand you the key" and so forth.

Just remember to look for what people secretly hate.

NOTE: When applying this principle remember some people hate and love different things so always keep in mind who you are speaking to and exactly what kind of people you want to target.

Because, Because, Because

While writing, it's a good idea to keep imagining the reader asking why and start answering a lot of those questions starting with the word "because".

However, once the copy is finished, a lot of the instances where I use the word "because' can come out and make great spots to break up or shorten sentences.

For example, let's suppose we are selling a particular brand of organic blueberries and the unique hook is they are grown on land which has never seen a drop of pesticide.

In telling the story I may write...

First Draft

> Billy's Blueberries are prized among the most picky health food lovers.
>
> The Chiles family has and always will keep the land free of such toxins.

After Explaining Why Using "Because"

> Billy's Blueberries are prized among the most picky health food lovers because they are grown on land that has never seen a drop of pesticide because Indians who would never use harmful chemicals gave the land to the ex-governor of Florida because they knew he would be a good shepherd of that piece of earth.
>
> The Chiles family has and always will keep the land free of toxic pesticides.

Final Draft After Removing "Because"

> Billy's Blueberries are prized among the most picky health food lovers.
>
> Billy's juicy dark blueberries are grown on land which has never seen a drop of pesticide.
>
> You see, the American Indians who would never use harmful chemicals to grow crops gave 200 acres to the ex-Governor of Florida knowing he would be a good shepherd of that piece of earth.
>
> The Chiles family who owns the farm which grows Billy's blueberries has and always will keep the land free of toxic pesticides.

Hidden Psychology To
Make People Chase Your Offer

Many of the techniques I have explained so far use hidden psychology to get the prospect to decide to read your copy and then keep them reading but this next psychological trick is designed to make your potential customers chase your offer.

There are lots of theories about how our very complicated brains work but we do know the most base level response we humans have is what they call the flight or fight instinct.

Throughout all of human history, those who knew when to run toward food or run away from danger lived and prospered more than those who froze with indecision.

Because of this, almost everyone alive today comes from ancestors with the fight or flight instinct in their DNA.

This is why the first thing every human subconsciously asks themselves when confronted with anything new is "do I want this?" or "should I fear this?".

A pile of cash immediately causes a gut reaction of desire.

A house on fire causes us to immediately assess the threat to our lives but this doesn't mean you have to show girls in bikinis or brutal thugs to take advantage of this base level flight or fight instinct we all have.

Yes, an attractive woman can increase results dramatically but that isn't really the third level of psychology I am about to show you.

To prompt most people to take action we need to be forced to make a decision.

Motivation to act can be sparked in many different ways but it is always a fear of missing out on something good or a fear of the consequences for not acting.

This is why I teach marketers to try and add some sense of urgency to their promotions but we can use this fight or flight instinct to punch up copy by making one simple change.

I'm going to explain how to give your copy a sense of a movement so they get the feeling they may miss out on something good or get into danger if they delay paying attention to the copy or making a buying decision but first... I have to remind you of a basic English lesson.

If you recall all words are categorized as nouns, verbs, pronouns, adjectives, adverbs etc.

The verbs are action words and most writing is written in the past tense.

In this next example I have underlined all the verbs.

Sample:

The Halbert Copywriting Method TM <u>has taken</u> many copywriters to the next level and <u>added</u> an extra digit to their take-home pay.

The word "taken" makes it past tense because it describes something which has already happened.

Now let's change that to the copywriter's favorite tense, present progressive which means the verb indicates the action is ongoing.

Basically every word ending in "ING" is progressive and if it indicates it is happening now, it is called present progressive.

With the exception of stories, I like to use the present progressive wherever possible.

For example, here is that line again except we have used the present progressive or version of the words ending with "ing" to create a sense of ongoing movement.

The Halbert Copywriting Method TM is taking many copywriters to the next level and adding an extra digit to their take-home pay.

It may seem like an insignificant little difference but over a paragraph or two you can really change the perception of the prospect in a way which makes them act and here's why.

When you hear that a product has sold very well your brain starts to get curious why other humans are so interested.

When you hear that a product is selling many copies right now you still feel curious but you also feel a need for enough information to make a quicker decision because you may miss out if demand drives the price up or they run out.

And... ongoing movements are always more exciting and attention getting.

Web Formatting

There are some important differences in how you should edit copy to be used in different medias.

For example, you don't have to worry about sentence length when it comes to writing scripts which will be spoken and read by the viewer.

If you stick with editing for print which is what we have been covering in this book you should be good to go for all medias but...

It's important to note that web pages can be formatted to hide a lot of the copy in such a way the user can expand and dive deeper into the information that really interests them.

There is a long standing argument among copywriters about long vs. short copy.

As we covered earlier, the shorter copy appears to be, the easier it is for the reader to decide to start reading.

Really long copy can make the prospect think "I really don't have time to read this now" and when it comes to sales, delay is death.

People mean to get back to all kinds of things they never get around to later.

On the other hand sometimes it takes a lot of copy to sell a product or service.

With copy posted online you can put all the most interesting and enticing statements on the page and make it so the user can click to see more details and information about what excites them.

This allows you to make a very long piece of sales copy appear very short.

In some cases advertisers make the statements links which take the prospects to different pages with more details but I prefer leaving all the copy on one page and using the links to expand the copy so the reader never feels lost in a website or has to go back to the main page to see the next exciting feature or benefit.

Here is an example.

Top Copywriter Flooding Businesses With New Customers Using Simple & <u>Free</u> 3 - Step Formula!

Los Angeles California- While most ad agencies are done selling once a client has signed a contract, one top copywriter is helping small businesses tap into the power of his three-step plan to get a steady stream of new customers before business owners spend a dime.

His name is Bond Halbert and if you recognize the last name it's because his father was widely considered to be the best ad writer in history but the younger Mr. Halbert comes with a lot more than just a pedigree in marketing.

Few people on Earth know as much about effective ad writing as Bond Halbert and... nobody else started learning how to create winning marketing campaigns at an earlier age. <u>Read More...</u>

With a lot of success in his own resume Bond Halbert is continuing the family tradition of providing small business owners with powerful and proven marketing they would not be able to afford without men like Bond and his father giving back and he has been sharing his 3 step formula absolutely free for more than a year.

The first step is to get current customers to answer a few simple questions to determine what really gets them to buy.

He also shows owners how to make customers glad to answer his 5 basic questions during a free online training session. <u>Click To Read More About the 5 Questions</u>

The second step is to select 3-5 easy marketing plans you can test for little to no money out of 20 proven campaign strategies. <u>Click Here To Read More About The 20 Strategies</u>

The third step is to use the funds from successful tests to grow a large marketing campaign to flood your business with new customers and then make those customers happy to

Now with the use of expandable text, I could add pages and pages of copy to explain my credentials. I can add pages and pages of benefits and features of the online workshop and I can make a lot of arguments about how small business owners can't lose by attending a free online workshop.

The next page shows what the sales copy looks like once someone has clicked all the links which expand the copy but don't take the reader to an order page.

Top Copywriter Is Flooding Businesses With New Customers Using Simple & <u>Free</u> 3 - Step Formula!

Los Angeles California- While most ad agencies are done selling once a client has signed a contract, one top copywriter is helping small businesses tap into the power of his three-step plan to get a steady stream of new customers before business owners spend a dime.

His name is Bond Halbert and if you recognize the last name it's because his father was widely considered to be the best ad writer in history but the younger Mr. Halbert comes with a lot more than just a pedigree in marketing.

Few people on Earth know as much about effective ad writing as Bond Halbert and nobody else started learning how to create winning marketing campaigns at an earlier age.

The now famous book The Boron Letters, captures Gary teaching his son how to craft brilliant promotions at a very young age because he recognized how quickly Bond grasped marketing concepts.

After working in the family business for many years Bond got a marketing degree and later returned to the world of direct response marketing because of the freedom it offered.

Soon his legendary father and Bond teamed up and this time, based on Bond's ideas and leadership, they built a company which raked in more money than even Gary Halbert ever made before.

At the time of his passing, Bond had built his own companies and then picked up the mantle of teaching aspiring copywriters how to put together winning ad campaigns.

With a lot of success in his own resume Bond Halbert is continuing the family tradition of providing small business owners with powerful and proven marketing they would not be able to afford without men like Bond and his father giving back and he has been sharing his 3 step formula absolutely free for more than a year.

The first step is to get current customers to answer a few simple questions to determine what really gets them to buy.

He also shows owners how to make customers glad to answer his 5 basic questions during a free online training session.

The sessions began in October of this year where Bond will show you how to create products that almost sell themselves by word of mouth alone.

Bond says it's hard enough to sell products and service people could really use and marketing is a lot easier if you can create offers the market is already screaming for.

The second step is to select 3-5 easy marketing plans you can test for little to no money out of 20 proven campaign strategies. Click Here To Read More About The 20 Strategies

The strategies have all been proven to work over decades but the key is choosing the strategies which match the market and the offer.

What information a customer needs to make a buying decision varies based on a lot of factors and the segment of market you are trying to reach.

You don't want to advertise local businesses through national media where the majority of the audience can't take advantage of even the best offers because you will be paying for what the industry pros calls waste circulation (people who would never buy those types of products).

You also can't sell a lot of houses using little classified ads because buyers require a lot more information than the space allows but...

If you get the right message to the right market through the right format you will make a lot of sales without spending a lot of time and money.

The third step is to use the funds from successful tests to grow a large marketing campaign to flood your business with new customers and then make those customers happy to spend more and help advertise the business.

The beauty of direct response marketing is each winning promotion adds profit to the business which can be reinvested to reach even larger segments of the market.

This eliminates the need for more investors and waiting years for a start-up to turn profitable which means you don't have to give up lots of control and money to grow your business.

Sound Too Good To Be True?

Mr. Halbert says, "the biggest problem with helping any small business is owners have been so disappointment by so many over-hyped marketing gurus, it's hard to believe anyone would offer such help for free" but...

Fortunately the Halbert family has a very long and well proven track record of helping small businesses get big business strategies that a simple online search proves this is for real.

Bond continues to provide real world actionable advice through TheGaryHalbertLetter.com and BondHalbert.com but a simple Google search will bring up many podcasts and videos where you will clearly see he is not only well respected for having one of the most innovative minds in the business.

Often referred to as marketing royalty the Halbert family enjoys an unparalleled reputation for providing the very best marketing advice.

Plus, since getting started is absolutely free, all you risk is an hour of your time and the upside is the kind of financial freedom most people can only dream about.

If you or someone you know owns a small to medium size

> small businesses explode with new customers but hurry.
>
> As Mr. Halbert says. "there are only so many hours in the day and I have to limit free help to around 30 businesses a month and the appointment book is filling up fast." <u>Click Here For More Details</u>
>
> PS If you don't get a spot in the program you can still get a lot of great tips for growing your business free at <u>halbertising.com</u>

While writing this book I chose to cover subjects in the order they should be learned but not in the order in which these ideas should be implemented in your copy.

As you start editing you will do things like break up paragraphs and look for pronouns to replace at the same time.

Soon you will use fewer pronouns in your writing but you will still want to use a checklist to make sure you haven't forgotten to do things like remove words like "learn" or punch up the testimonials using ellipses.

In fact you want to use checklists throughout the entire copywriting process.

You can get a copy of my promotional checklist which will make sure you have added a takeaway, testimonials, a sense of urgency and all the other elements you should consider putting in your sales copy.

To make sure you can't forget a step, I have put together an editing checklist but you must know... the checklist is not in the same order the steps are covered in the book for a reason.

You can apply the steps in any order you see fit but this is roughly the order I think these steps should be taken to save you time.

For example indenting non-dynamic copy and breaking up long paragraphs are covered in the same section on formatting but it saves time to indent paragraphs after you have finished rearranging sentences to leave the reader wanting more.

More Resources / Editing Tools

TheGaryHalbertLetter.com- No website has ever done more for the copywriting industry than TheGaryHalbertLetter.com

Here you will find the best instructions and "fun to read" content on learning how to write great copy.

The letters have inspired, launched, and improved the careers of countless professional copywriters all over the world and their popularity is still growing.

If you have spent any time learning how to write copy you will have an ah-ha moment when you realize this is THE place where most, if not all, of the so called direct marketing geniuses, mentors, and coaches learned their craft even if they didn't give credit to the Prince of Print himself.

As one of the greatest professional copywriters alive today put it- "In the world of copywriting ALL roads lead back to Gary Halbert" and it is true.

TheGaryHalbertLetter.com is the copywriting equivalent of Mecca, The Temple Mount, and Church Of The Holy Sepulchre in Jeruselum all rolled into one.

If you haven't been to TheGaryHalbertLetter.com this has to be your next stop to get more effective copywriting skills.

http://bondhalbert.com/- At this site you will learn more techniques few other copywriting coaches share simply because they don't know them. I have spent decades reading the best copy ever written and I not only recognize the patterns nobody else discusses I share with you unique and simple tactics you can put to use in your own writing to make more sales.

This is the site you will find copywriting news, hot new research tips, and better ways to apply persuasion techniques before the ideas and concepts are stolen by others.

Hemingway App- The Hemingway app is a great tool for checking the readability and grade level of your writing. Remember, you will never get criticism because what you explained was too simple or too easy to understand and this app will help undo any damage done by your high school English teachers.

Thesaurus.com- Any Thesaurus will do but it is so handy to have such resources online so you can find more simple and easy words for clarity.

NationalEnquirer.com- Sometimes you are looking for a thrilling hook and over the top way of starting a point and The National Enquirer has been wording headlines to get maximum attention for decades. Buzz words like "Epic" and "Amazing" will come and go and return again but the folks over at The Enquirer are always on top of what's gripping readers attention right now so it is a great resource for learning such language.

Thank You Page

No one person does it all alone and I am no exception.

I'd like to give a very special thanks to the many people who have helped with the creation of this book and I'd like to express my sincerest gratitude to the good people who have supported the entire Halbert family over the years.

Let's start with the folks who have been especially helpful in getting this book ready to print.

First and foremost I must thank my father Gary Halbert. His influence can be seen in everything I do because he took the time to teach me how to think like he did. I love you pop and I as per your instructions I will always credit you for anything I do well and protect you from the blame for anything I do wrong.

I of course have to give credit to one of the brains behind the entire family who cracked the code on making our father's first major success and taught us all to go for it and I'm of course talking about my mother Nancy Halbert.

I'd like to thank Benny Valenzuela, Rae Brent, Pauline Longdon, Lorrie Morgan-Ferrero, James Schramko, Michael Lofton, Lawton Chiles, and Nader Anise for being my second sets of eyes and giving me such valuable feedback.

I'd also like to give Jake Szaraz the credit he deserves for his help with the cover.

Sam Markowitz was very helpful in inspiring me to put my ideas out in the world and I can't thank him enough for always being a great sounding board to bounce ideas off of. I'm the go to guy for ideas for many marketers and you are my go to guy.

My brother Kevin Halbert deserves credit for letting me take the time from our joint ventures to put this book together and getting over his fear that I will tarnish the family name which is almost a 100% certainty.

I of course would also like to thank my wife and our kids Emma and Preston. They are the reason I care about the future.

Printed in Great Britain
by Amazon